24-

THE CASE OF
The Sneezy Popcorn

Michelle Faulk, PhD

Enslow Publishers, Inc.
40 Industrial Road
Box 398
Berkeley Heights, NJ 07922
USA

http://www.enslow.com

Library of Congress Cataloging-in-Publication Data

Faulk, Michelle

    The case of the sneezy popcorn : Annie Biotica solves respiratory system disease crimes / by
      Michelle Faulk.
        p. cm. — (Body system disease investigations)
      Summary: "Learn about strep throat, Hantavirus, whooping cough, Pneumonia, and the
      differences between the cold and the flu. Then try to guess the disease in three different
      cases"— Provided by publisher.
    Includes index.
    ISBN 978-0-7660-3946-9
    1. Cold (Disease)—Juvenile literature. 2. Influenza—Juvenile literature. I. Title.
    RF361.F38 2012
    616.2'05—dc23   2011013523

Future editions:
Paperback ISBN 978-1-4644-0228-9
ePUB ISBN 978-1-4645-1141-7
PDF ISBN 978-1-4646-1141-4

Printed in China
062012 Leo Paper Group, Heshan City, Guangdong, China

10 9 8 7 6 5 4 3 2 1

Photo Credits: AP Images/Jens Meyer, p. 35; CDC: Cynthia Goldsmith, p. 16 (top), 19 (top), D. Loren Ketai, M.D., p. 15 (top), Dr. J.J. Farmer, p. 31; Dr. Richard Facklam, p. 30 (middle); Enslow Publishers, Inc., p. 43; Jeff Weigel, www.jeffweigel.com, pp. 1, 3, 5, 9, 13, 14, 19, 21, 25, 27, 31, 33, 37, 38, 40, 42, 47; Pixland/Photos.com, p. 15 (middle); Photo Researchers, Inc.: A. Barry Dowsett, pp. 22, 24 (bottom), Dr. P. Marazzi, p. 9 (top), Eye of Science, pp. 29 (top), 39 (bottom), Hank Morgan, p. 30 (bottom), NIBSC, p. 23 (top), Pasieka, pp. 33 (left), 34, 36, PHANIE, p. 11, Roger Harris, p. 27, Scott Camazine, pp. 28, 38, 40; Shutterstock.com, pp. 7, 9 (bottom), 10, 12, 13 (top, middle), 15 (bottom), 16 (bottom), 17, 18, 19 (bottom), 20, 21, 23 (bottom), 24 (top), 29 (bottom), 30 (top), 32, 33 (right), 39 (top), 41, 44, and all checkmark and magnifying glass graphics.

Cover Illustration: Jeff Weigel, www.jeffweigel.com

Contents

Test Alex's Blood

Alex had been exposed to mice infected with hantavirus. Was Alex infected? I took a sample of Alex's blood and tested it to see if it contained antibodies against the hantavirus. Antibodies are Y-shaped proteins made by the body's immune system. They grab invaders and hold them down for elimination. Each antibody recognizes only one invader.

Results: Alex's blood did contain antibodies that recognized hantavirus. This was proof that the virus had entered and attacked Alex's body.

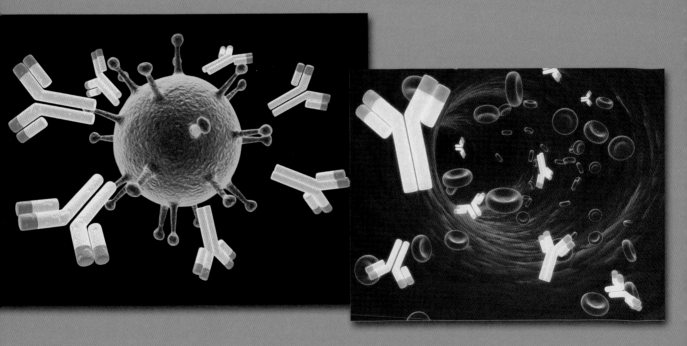

Hantavirus antibodies were found in Alex's blood.

The Verdict

It was now clear that the hantavirus was the culprit in this case. This virus was found guilty on all counts.

CONVICTED GERM
Hantavirus

Justice

Viruses are notoriously hard to get rid of and hantavirus is one of the worst. To help Alex I called in backup. Other people have been attacked by hantavirus and survived to tell the tale. Their blood now contained valuable antibodies. Many of these disease crime survivors donated their antibodies to treat people like Alex. It took over a month but Alex did get better.

Protective clothing, a respirator, and gloves can protect you when you are working near animals that may be infected with hantavirus.

This is Agent Annie Biotica signing off. Stay safe out there.

Chapter 3

Whooping Cough and THE CASE OF the 100-Day Cough

The Crime

This case involved a young woman who was a world champion athlete. Dori had been sick for weeks. She had a horrible cough.

Her doctor told her she had bronchitis. This happens when the bronchial tubes swell. Less air can

get in and out of the lungs. Many microbes can cause bronchitis. But this isn't usually a serious disease. Most people are able to fight off their microbial attackers on their own. When Dori continued to get sicker, I was called in.

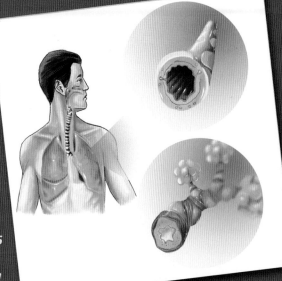

Bronchitis occurs when disease criminals cause the bronchial tubes in the lungs to swell. This swelling prevents air from getting in and out of the lungs.

The Clues

When I saw Dori she had these symptoms:

- Headaches and a low fever
- A cough that kept getting worse
- Aches and tiredness
- After four weeks Dori was experiencing about fifteen coughing attacks each day. Many times she vomited afterwards. She was exhausted and her chest and stomach muscles were very sore.

The Suspects

Bronchitis can cause these symptoms. But Dori should have fought off a bronchitis attack by now. What bothered me was how severe her cough was. The coughing came in bursts and they were so powerful she couldn't catch her breath. As I listened closely I got an important clue. When she was finally able to take in a breath after a coughing fit, Dori made a very clear "whoop" sound. (See page 47 for a site where you can hear what whooping cough sounds like.) That sound told me Dori probably had whooping cough.

Whooping cough is caused by a witch of a germ named *Bordetella pertussis*, or *B. pertussis* for short. This germ criminal enjoys attacking kids. Only once in a while does it work up the nerve to attack an adult.

In addition to helping Dori, I feared for public safety. Dori could unknowingly infect a lot of people. Many of those could be babies. Eighty percent of babies who get whooping cough die. It was important to determine if *B. pertussis* was the culprit in this crime and to quickly lock it up.

The Evidence

Test One Polymerase Chain Reaction (PCR)

B. pertussis are very small but extremely nasty bacteria. These bad girls like to cause a lot of damage. They produce a poison

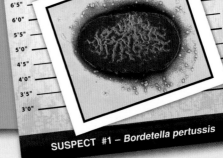

SUSPECT #1 – *Bordetella pertussis*

Cilia of the respiratory system are being attacked by Bordetella pertussis *(shown in lime green).*

that kills a person's cilia. Cilia, which are found on some cells, are like tiny hairs that sweep mucus up and out. Without them the mucus continues to build up. The coughing spells get violent as the body desperately tries to force the mucus out.

To try and identify *B. pertussis* as the culprit, I had Dori cough into a sterile cup. I took the mucus she coughed up and performed two tests.

Because the PCR test is so sensitive, I tested some of Dori's mucus to see if it contained *B. pertussis*.

Results: The PCR test for *B. pertussis* was positive.

The PCR test showed that Dori's mucus contained B. *pertussis.*

Test Two

Grow the Bacteria

The PCR test is very specific. But since *B. pertussis* is such a dangerous disease, I needed two positive IDs. I did a second laboratory line-up by trying to grow *B. pertussis* from Dori's mucus. I took some of Dori's mucus and spread it on agar containing sheep's blood and potatoes. This is a favorite food of *B. pertussis*. Live *B. pertussis* was present in Dori's mucus.

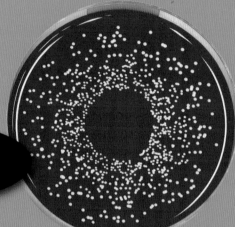

Dori's mucus had *B. pertussis* in it.

The Verdict

Both the PCR and agar tests were positive for *B. pertussis*. These results told me without a doubt that Dori had whooping cough. *B. pertussis* was found guilty on all counts and sentenced to be eliminated.

CONVICTED GERM
Bordetella pertussis

Justice

The standard treatment for whooping cough is antibiotics. Dori's husband and young son were also given antibiotics to protect them against infection. It took over a month, but Dori slowly got better.

A Hard Criminal to Contain

B. pertussis is extremely contagious. These bacteria like to hit a victim, multiply, and then move on to new victims fast. Until Dori was completely better she had to be very careful to keep this disease criminal contained. She had to constantly wash her hands, throw her used tissues in the garbage, and not share cups or dishes with anyone. She had to stay home and keep away from other people, especially children. Dori's 100-day cough was a tough case. It was pretty scary to think of how many people may have been hurt if that bacterium had rioted around the city.

This is Agent Annie Biotica signing off. Stay safe out there.

Chapter 4

Pneumonia *and* THE CASE OF *the* Squishy Lungs

The Crime

Ming Ling was a forty-year-old woman who had been attacked by a very stubborn germ criminal. She had been fighting a sinus infection for nearly a year. She kept going to the doctor, but antibiotics just didn't seem to work. Then one day she felt so sick she couldn't take it anymore. She headed to the emergency room. That's when I got the call.

When Ming got to the ER she had these symptoms:

* Fever
* Chills
* Fatigue
* Shortness of breath
* Coughing up brown mucus
* Chest pain

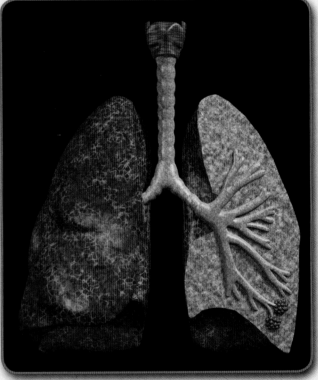

The alveoli are in the lungs, shown as the small, round, pink areas.

The two symptoms Ming had that really worried me were the brown mucus and chest pain. Mucus is often brown when it contains dead red blood cells. Bacteria like to kill red blood cells. Chest pain indicates damage down deep in the lungs. I investigated further.

I listened to her lung sounds with a stethoscope. When she breathed I heard crackling sounds that are called rales. It's like the sound of hair rubbing between your fingers. Rales mean that the alveoli are clogged. This is more evidence of a deep lung infection.

I sent Ming to get a chest X-ray. One side of Ming's lungs had a white cloudy look to it. This meant fluid. The fluid was making it hard for Ming to breathe. Fluid in the lungs can mean pneumonia. But what microbial culprit was causing the pneumonia?

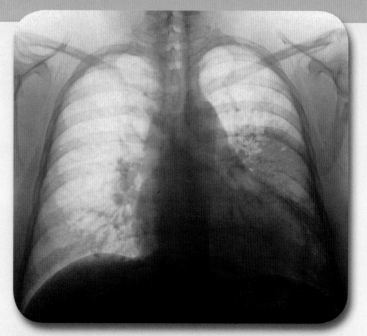

The liquid in Ming's lungs was evidence of pneumonia (shown in blue).

The Suspects

Pneumonia can be caused by bacteria and viruses. Ming's brown mucus pointed to a bacterial suspect. It was very possible the mischievous bacterial character that had been hiding out in her sinuses decided to visit her lungs. The primary suspect was *Streptococcus pneumoniae*. He is well known for causing sinus infections and pneumonia. This was the microbe I decided to go after.

The Case of the Sneezy Popcorn

The Evidence

Test One — The Gram Stain

SUSPECT - The Gram positive *Streptococci* found in Ming's mucus.

I had Ming cough up some mucus into a sterile container. I took some of the mucus sample and spread it on a microscope slide. I then did a Gram stain. This chemical test helps divide the many bacteria that exist into two categories. If they stain purple they are Gram positive and if they stain red they are Gram negative. Also, by staining the bacteria I can better see their shape and size. *Streptococcus* bacteria are Gram positive, round, and form chains.

Results: Ming's mucus contained Gram positive bacteria that were round and in chains and pairs. Now I knew the bacteria causing Ming's disease was a member of the *Streptococcus* crime family. But was it *Streptococcus pneumoniae*?

First I needed a lot of bacteria to run this test. I grew more of the bacteria from Ming's mucus on blood agar. After the bacteria grew, I saw clear areas where the blood cells had been killed. This was an early indication that this bacteria was *S. pneumoniae*.

This agar plate shows bacteria that grew out of Ming's mucus. The clear area around the bacteria indicate this is *Streptococcus pneumoniae*.

Test Two — The Antibody Test

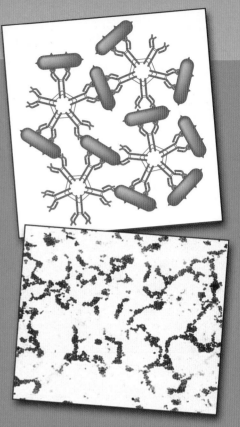

I put samples of the bacteria into test tubes. I added antibodies that had been specifically made against *S. pneumoniae*. Quickly all the bacteria clumped together and sank to the bottom of the tube. Under a microscope I confirmed that the *S. pneumoniae* antibodies had linked the *S. pneumoniae* together into clumps.

Results: The antibody test was positive for *S. pneumoniae*.

The S. pneumoniae antiboidies linked to the bacteria. This caused them to clump together (as shown below, under the microscope).

The Verdict

There was now no doubt. Ming Ling had pneumonia that was caused by the bacterium *Streptococcus pneumoniae*. *S. pneumoniae* was found guilty on all counts and sentenced to be eliminated.

CONVICTED GERM
S. pneumoniae

Justice

Ming was given the antibiotic penicillin to kill the *S. pneumoniae* in her system. I felt good watching Ming leave the hospital and return home to recover.

The Criminal Escapes!

Two weeks later I got a call. Ming was back at the hospital! The antibiotics hadn't worked and she was still very sick. I raced down there.

At the hospital I went over the case again. Had I missed something? Then I remembered that Ming had been on several antibiotics for the last year because of her sinus infection. One of these was penicillin. Disease scene investigators around the world had been coming up against bacteria that were not being killed by antibiotics. These are called drug-resistant bacteria. Maybe the *S. pneumoniae* in Ming's system had become drug-resistant.

I took a fresh mucus sample from Ming and spread it on an agar plate not containing red blood cells. Then I put down small paper discs containing different antibiotics. After the bacteria had time to grow it was clear that the *S. pneumoniae* in Ming's lungs was resistant to penicillin. The bacteria had grown right up to the penicillin disc. It wasn't afraid of that drug at all. Lucky for Ming, this test showed us that there were antibiotics her *S. pneumoniae* was sensitive to. Around the paper disc containing amoxicillin there was a definite clear zone. This was the antibiotic that the doctor prescribed for Ming. Two weeks later her illness had greatly improved.

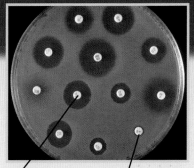

Ming's S. pnuemoniae culture shows antibiotic discs. It is clear that this bacteria is resistant to penicillin.

Amoxicillin disc

Penicillin disc

This is Agent Annie Biotica signing off. Stay safe out there.

Pneumonia and the Case of the Squishy Lungs

Chapter 5

WAS IT A *Cold* OR THE *Flu?*

The Crime

Children in the early 1900s would sing this song while jumping rope: "I had a little bird, his name was Enza. I opened the window and in-flu-enza."

The infamous germ criminal influenza virus has been on our Ten Most Wanted list for as long as I can remember. Influenza is a virus that causes a contagious respiratory illness called the flu. Why is this bug so hard to catch? Because influenza reinvents himself each year by creating a new disguise while hiding out in Asia. From Asia he travels through Europe, North America, and then ends his path of destruction in South America.

For most people, the flu is just an awful and inconvenient thing to experience. But for older people and those in poor health, it can kill. Flu can also be tough to ID. He is often mistaken for the many viruses that cause a different respiratory disease called a "cold". Take for example the case of a girl named Mayada. Her mother was very worried that Mayada may be a victim of the influenza virus. I went immediately to investigate.

The Clues

Mayada was lying in bed and obviously feeling very sick. Her symptoms had come on very suddenly the day before. They included:

- A fever of 102°F.
- Muscle aches and pains all over her body. Mayada said she felt like a big gorilla had stomped all over her.
- She was extremely tired.
- A mild cough.

The Suspects

The flu and colds have similar symptoms because they both attack the respiratory system. To solve Mayada's case I used the scientific method. I logically followed the evidence to see what conclusion it would bring me to.

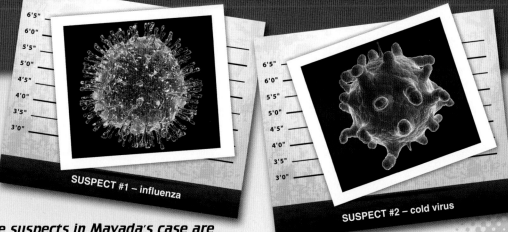

SUSPECT #1 – influenza

SUSPECT #2 – cold virus

The suspects in Mayada's case are the influenza and cold viruses.

Did Mayada have a cough?
Yes: This could indicate either flu or cold.

Was Mayada coughing up yellow or green mucus?
No: This verifies that the infection is most likely viral and not bacterial.
Influenza and cold viruses are still the suspects.

Did Mayada have a sore throat?
Yes: While colds always cause sore throats, they are sometimes seen in cases
of the flu. Influenza and cold viruses are still the suspects.

Did Mayada's symptoms come on suddenly?
Yes: This indicates the flu more than a cold. Cold symptoms take time to build
up while flu symptoms appear suddenly. Influenza is now the main suspect.

Did Mayada have a lot of muscle aches and was she extremely tired?
Yes: These are classic symptoms of the flu and are not usually seen in cases of
a cold attack. More evidence that influenza is the culprit.

Did Mayada have a fever?
Yes, and a high one: This is more evidence of the influenza virus. Fevers are
rarely seen in cold attacks.

Some of Mayada's symptoms strongly pointed
to influenza. Her illness came on suddenly,
she had bad muscle aches, she was very
tired, and she had a high fever. I visited
Mayada's school. I found out that many of her
classmates were sick with similar symptoms.
Influenza germs are famous for hitting a lot
of people at once. This is called an epidemic.
If this was a flu epidemic I needed solid
laboratory evidence to close the case.

Flu is now the main suspect.

The Evidence

Test One — The Rapid Influenza Test

Doctors can now test for influenza right in their office. These tests are called rapid influenza diagnostic tests, or RIDTs for short. I used long cotton swabs to take samples from Mayada's nose and throat. I used these samples in the prepackaged influenza test. If a color reaction occurs, Mayada has the flu.

Mayada's samples were positive for influenza virus.

Based on Mayada's symptoms and the RIDT, the influenza virus was found guilty of attacking this little girl. Because antibiotics do not work on viruses, another punishment was necessary. Mayada's doctor gave her an antiviral medicine.

CONVICTED GERM
Influenza virus

Case Closed, or Was It?

I got a call a week later from Mayada's mother. Mayada was still complaining of a sore throat. I had tested her and found her negative for having strep throat. Did I make a mistake? Had she been attacked by a second germ criminal while recovering from her flu? I made a visit to Mayada's home.

I found Mayada still in bed. This was not unexpected. Even with the antivirals it will take time for Mayada to get all her strength back. She took a break from eating ice cream to let me have a look at her throat. It looked very healthy. While her mother went to get more ice cream I talked with Mayada. She confessed a secret. Whenever she has a sore throat her mother gives her all the ice cream she wants. Mayada had been fibbing to keep getting lots of ice cream. Lying to a disease investigator is a serious crime, but I decided to let her go with just a warning. I explained to Mayada how important it was to tell the truth about disease symptoms. I also told her that after the next bowl of ice cream she needed to tell her mother that her throat felt fine.

This is Agent Annie Biotica signing off. Stay safe out there.

Jacob's grandmother had come to stay with his family because she didn't feel well. She was coughing and sneezing and his mother wanted to take care of her.

One day Jacob decided to play a joke on Grandma. He put his pet rat Pete in her bed. He had gotten Pete at a pet store two years ago and he was very friendly. Jacob hid in the closet when Grandma went to bed. He couldn't help laughing when Grandma screamed and jumped out of bed. The fun was soon over when Jacob saw a little blood on Grandma's hand. It seemed that Pete the rat had been just as scared as Grandma. He had bitten her.

Several days after the joke, Grandma's illness got worse. She was coughing a lot more. The mucus that she was coughing out was brown. When she started to have trouble breathing Jacob's parents took her to the hospital.

The doctors X-rayed Grandma's lungs. They saw liquid in her lungs.

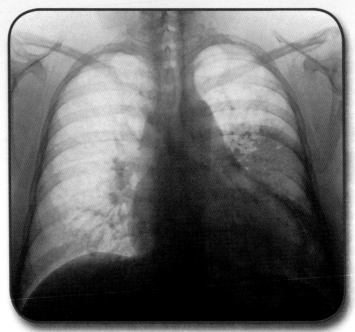

Grandma's chest X-ray shows a blue area where there is liquid in her lung.

A sample of Grandma's mucus after it grew on a blood agar plate for 24 hours. The bacteria killed the red blood cells in the agar.

The doctors took some of Grandma's mucus and put it on a blood agar plate overnight. This is what it looked like. The bacteria that grew popped the blood cells in the agar.

The doctors also took some of the bacteria from the blood agar plate and did a Gram stain. They found a lot of Gram positive bacteria.

The doctors put Grandma on strong antibiotics. After ten days of antibiotic treatment Grandma felt a lot better.

1. Do you think Grandma had gotten hantavirus from Pete the rat biting her?

2. Grandma's cough was never bad enough that she vomited. She also never made a whooping noise. What does this tell you?

3. A lung X-ray also showed a lot of liquid in her lungs. The bacteria that grew from Grandma's mucus killed red blood cells. The bacteria were Gram positive. What disease do you think Grandma may have had?

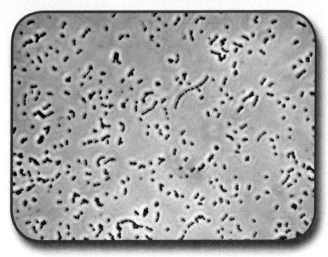

There was Gram positive bacteria in Grandma's mucus.

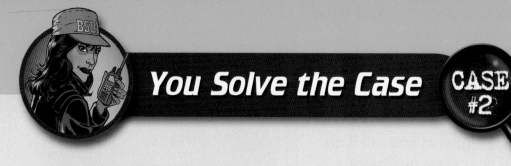

Five-year-old Akhil woke up one morning and started to cry. All he could tell his father was that his mouth hurt. At the doctor's office they found that Akhil had a temperature of 104°F. When the doctor went to examine Akhil's throat he immediately noticed his breath smelled like rotten food. He also saw that Akhil's throat was very red. There were also small white spots on the inside of his mouth. When the doctor felt Akhil's neck he noticed swollen lymph nodes.

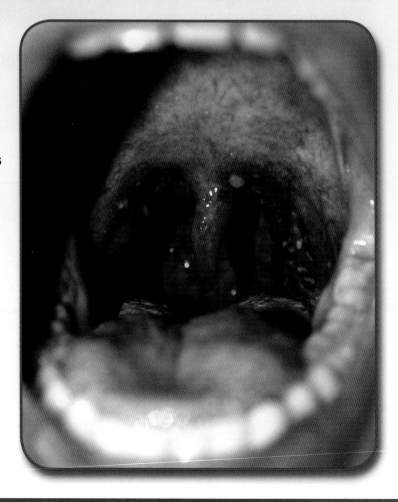

Akhil's mouth and throat

Akhil's throat sample on blood agar after 24 hours

1. Here is what the doctor's test results showed: The blood agar plate test was positive for *Streptococcus* bacteria but the rapid strep test was negative. Should he prescribe antibiotics?

2. If the doctor had determined that Akhil had a rhinovirus attack (a cold) what would the treatment have been?

You Solve the Case

CASE #3

A sixteen-year-old girl named Jennifer started to feel ill one weekend. Over the following week she gradually felt worse. Jennifer really wanted to go to a concert with her friends on Saturday. Her mother couldn't decide if she should let Jennifer go. She took Jennifer to a doctor on Friday. Here is what the doctor saw.

* Jennifer was sneezing a lot.

* Jennifer had a sore throat. This clue could indicate a cold or flu. A sore throat is a common symptom of a cold but is only sometimes seen with a flu attack.

* Jennifer had a mild cough. This clue points to a cold. Coughs can be seen in both cold and flu attacks. However, a flu cough is usually more severe.

* Jennifer's symptoms got worse gradually. This clue indicates a cold attack. A flu attack comes on more suddenly.

* Jennifer did not have a fever. This clue points to a cold. Fevers do happen in cold attacks, but they are usually rare. They always happen in a flu attack.

* Jennifer had some body aches and pains but she was still up and walking around. This clue points to a cold. If Jennifer had the flu she would feel like she had been hit by a bus.

* Jennifer was a little tired but she was still going to school and getting her homework done. This clue points to a cold. If Jennifer had the flu she would have been too tired to leave her bed.

1. Do you think Jennifer had the flu or a cold?
2. Is there a treatment for Jennifer's attack?

This is a chart of Jennifer's symptoms and whether they fit a cold or the flu.

Jennifer's Symptoms	Cold	Flu
Sneezing	Common	Sometimes
Sore Throat	Common	Sometimes
Cough	Mild	Severe
Symptoms Developed	Gradually	Suddenly
Fever	Sometimes	Always
Body Aches	Mild	Severe
Fatigue	Mild	Severe

CASE #1 Pneumonia

✳ **1.** *Do you think Grandma had gotten hantavirus from Pete the rat biting her?* No. Pete was not a wild rat and most likely had never been exposed to hantavirus. Also, Grandma was sick before she was bitten by Pete. Finally, antibiotics helped her get better. Antibiotics would not have had any effect on hantavirus.

✳ **2.** *Grandma's cough was never bad enough that she vomited. She also never made a whooping noise. What does this tell you?* That Grandma did not have whooping cough.

✳ **3.** *A lung X-ray also showed a lot of liquid in her lungs. The bacteria that grew from Grandma's mucus popped red blood cells. The same bacteria were Gram positive. What disease do you think Grandma may have had?* Bacterial pneumonia. Mucus that is brown is that color because of blood and dead cells. This is usually an indication of a bacterial infection. This was shown to be true when bacteria were found in Grandma's mucus sample. A deep lung infection results in liquid accumulating in the lungs. This is why Grandma's X-ray showed blue areas.

✳ **1. *Here is what the doctor's test results showed: The blood agar plate test was positive for* Streptococcus *bacteria but the rapid strep test was negative. Should he prescribe antibiotics?*** Yes. The rapid strep test is sometimes wrong. Strep throat can lead to more serious and even deadly diseases. The doctor should definitely begin Akhil on antibiotics.

✳ **2. *If the doctor had determined that Akhil had a rhinovirus attack (a cold) what would the treatment have been?*** Nothing. Antibiotics do not kill viruses. A cold is not usually a serious disease and the victim's immune system will usually fight it off.

CASE #3 **Common Cold**

✳ **1. *Do you think Jennifer had the flu or a cold?*** All of Jennifer's symptoms point to a cold. She did not have more severe cough and a fever. She was not terribly tired; she was still going to school and getting her homework done. And upon review of the chart, there are more checkmarks in the cold column.

✳ **2. *Is there a treatment for Jennifer's attack?*** No. A cold is caused by any one of many viruses. There are antiviral medicines available. However, a cold is not a serious health attack. Usually, the body's immune system will eventually win the battle with a cold attacker.

Glossary

agar: A gelatin substance high in sugar and made from red algae. Gives bacteria a place to grow and food to eat.

antibiotics: Medicines that inhibit the growth of bacteria.

antivirals: Medicines that inhibit the growth of viruses.

drug-resistant bacteria: Bacteria that are not killed by some or all antibiotics.

Hantavirus Cardiopulmonary Syndrome (HCPS): The disease caused by the hantavirus.

lymph nodes: Tissues in the body that filter microbe invaders out of the bloodstream.

PCR primers: Small pieces of RNA or DNA that find and stick to the genetic material of a microbe.

pharyngitis: An infection of the pharynx by bacteria or viruses.

rapid strep test: Easy and fast test to detect *Streptococcus* bacteria in a patient.

Rapid Influenza Diagnostic Tests (RIDT): Easy and fast tests to detect influenza virus in a patient.

respirator: A safety device that fits over the nose and mouth and filters the air.

rhinoviruses: A very large group of viruses that infect the respiratory system.

strep throat: A disease caused by the bacterium *Streptococcus pyrogenes* that is limited to the throat.

ventilator machine: A machine that will pump oxygen into a person when he is unable to breathe on his own.

Landau, Elaine. *Strep Throat.* New York: Marshall Cavendish Children's Books, 2010.

Levy, Janey. *The World of Microbes: Bacteria, Viruses, and Other Microorganisms.* New York: Rosen Publishing, 2010.

Simon, Seymour. *Lungs: Your Respiratory System.* Glasgow: Collins Education, 2007.

Internet Addresses

The Centers for Disease Control and Prevention (CDC). "Pneumococcal Disease – Questions & Answers." <http://www.cdc.gov/vaccines/vpd-vac/pneumo/dis-faqs.htm>

WebMD. The Sounds of Coughing. <http://children.webmd.com/pertussis-whooping-cough-10/coughing-sounds>
Hear how different diseases cause different sounding coughs.

Index

The Case of the Sneezy Popcorn